Oceans

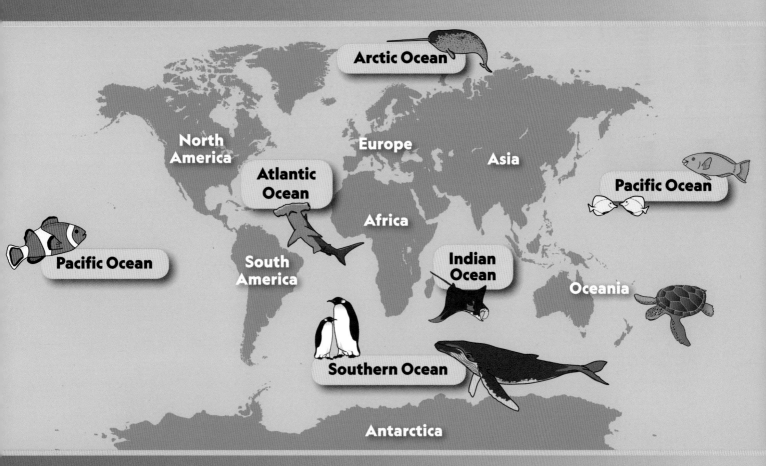

Arctic Ocean

North America

Europe

Asia

Atlantic Ocean

Pacific Ocean

Africa

Pacific Ocean

South America

Indian Ocean

Oceania

Southern Ocean

Antarctica

Find it! Explore it!

The Precious
PACIFIC OCEAN

The Pacific Ocean is the biggest ocean in the world. The Great Barrier Reef is found here. It is the world's largest reef and it is packed with many animals such as fish, sea turtles and seahorses as well as lots of colourful coral.

1 Pufferfish

2 Boxfish

3 Lion fish

4 Parrot fish

DID YOU KNOW?

The Great Barrier Reef is so big, it can be seen from outer space!

5 Porcupine fish

6 Surgeonfish

7 Anemones

8 Clownfish

CLOWNFISH AND SEA ANEMONE

Clownfish and sea anemones live together. A sea anemone has tentacles that sting most kinds of animals that come close to it. But it does not sting the clownfish. The anemone protects the clownfish from other fish that might want to eat it.

LET'S GO!

How many clownfish can you find on this page?

LET'S GO!

Look out for the magnifying glass hidden throughout the book. Collect the letters and unscramble them to spell an animal. Check your answer on page 47.

P

ANEMONES help protect clownfish and clownfish help feed sea anemones. This kind of relationship is called symbiosis.

LET'S GO!

Can you say 'symbiosis' (sim-bi-oh-sis)?

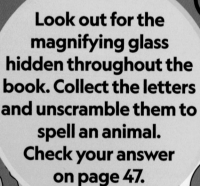

Explore it!

PORCUPINE FISH

Porcupine fish take big gulps of water to make themselves bigger. Most predators don't want to bite a big, prickly fish!

LIONFISH

Lionfish have spines filled with venom, which they use for protection. Lionfish are predators and usually hunt for food at night.

SURGEONFISH

Surgeonfish get their name because they have sharp spines near the base of their tails that are similar to scalpels (sharp tools used by surgeons as part of their job).

PARROTFISH

Parrotfish have strong beaks that they use to eat coral. They are very colourful fish. Their colour, shape and pattern can change throughout their lives. They can also change between being male and female.

PUFFERFISH

Pufferfish, also known as blowfish, are strange, scaleless fish that can 'puff' up to a much larger size. They're also very toxic!

LET'S GO!

Can you puff up like a pufferfish? Fill your cheeks with air and try not to laugh! Remember to breathe when you need to!

LET'S GO!

Like parrotfish, there are many sea creatures with other animals in their name. Can you think of any?

BOXFISH

Boxfish have a hard, boxy outer armour to protect themselves from predators. Some boxfish species have horns and are also known as 'cowfish'!

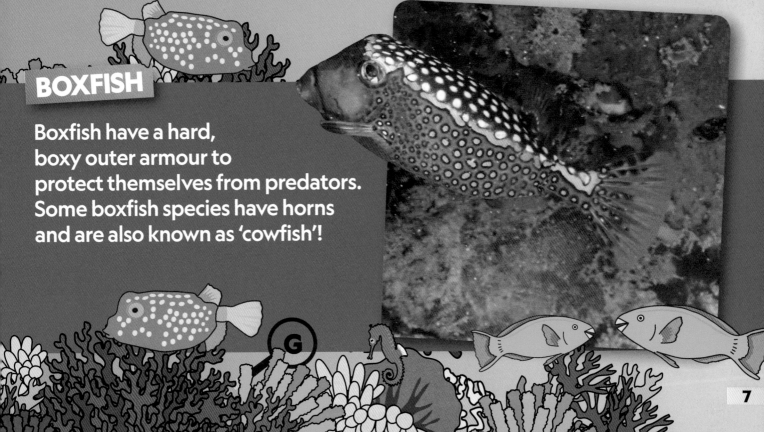

G

The Super
SOUTHERN OCEAN

The Southern Ocean is found around Antarctica. Antarctica is a frozen place that is unlike anywhere else on Earth. But with plenty of penguins and swooping albatrosses, there's so much life to discover...

1 Sperm whale

2 Humpback whales

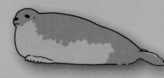

3 Weddell seals

4 Snow petrels

Find it!

DID YOU KNOW?

The coldest temperature on the planet was recorded here at –89 degrees celsius!

5 Wandering albatross

6 Southern elephant seals

7 Emperor penguins

8 Antarctic krill

EMPEROR PENGUIN

Emperor penguins are the world's largest penguins. They grow to 115 cm – about the same height as a six-year-old human. They gather in groups called colonies. The colonies are so big that they can be seen from space.

LET'S GO!

Can you waddle like a penguin from one side of the room to the other?

LET'S GO!

Blue whales like to eat lots of krill. What's your favourite food?

BLUE WHALES are the biggest animals on the planet! They have massive mouths with special filters that help them sieve their favourite food from the water.

Explore it!

WANDERING ALBATROSS

Wandering albatrosses are some of the biggest birds in the world and they can fly non-stop! They can live as long as 50 years in the wild and have wingspans of over 3 m!

LET'S GO!

If you could fly, where would you go and why?

SOUTHERN ELEPHANT SEAL

Southern elephant seals are the largest seals on Earth. They are called elephant seals because of their trunk-like snouts.

ANTARCTIC KRILL

Antarctic krill are like tiny little shrimp. They are one of the most important animals in the waters around Antarctica. This is because they are a food source for many animals that live there.

LET'S GO!

Can you think of any other creatures that jump out of the ocean?

HUMPBACK WHALE

Humpback whales do not actually have humps on their back. They get their name from the way that their back arches when they jump out of the water just before they dive.

ADÉLIE PENGUINS are one of the smallest penguin species in Antarctica. When diving into water to find food, they can hold their breath for up to six minutes.

SPERM WHALE

Sperm whales have the biggest brain of any creature on the planet. When hunting, sperm whales dive so deep that they hold their breath for around 90 minutes.

LET'S GO!

How long can you hold your breath for? Remember to stop if you feel dizzy!

WEDDELL SEAL

Weddell seals are born silver (their parents are grey). They can usually swim before they are two weeks old.

SNOW PETREL

Snow petrels are small birds – around the same size as a pigeon. They have pure white feathers, black eyes and a black beak.

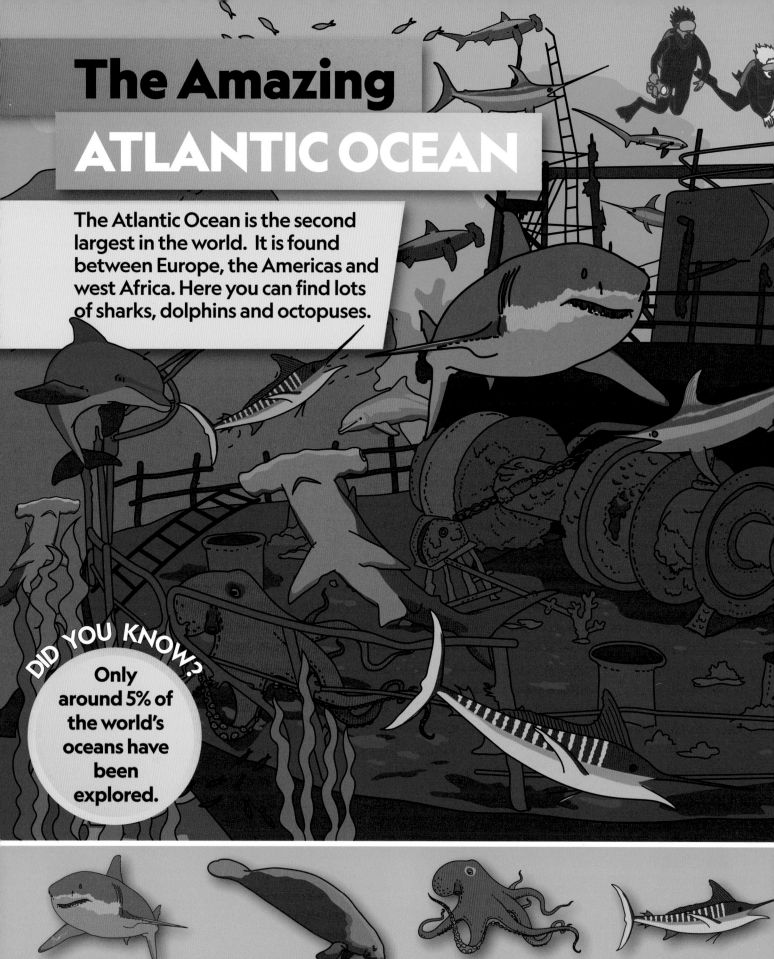

The Amazing
ATLANTIC OCEAN

The Atlantic Ocean is the second largest in the world. It is found between Europe, the Americas and west Africa. Here you can find lots of sharks, dolphins and octopuses.

DID YOU KNOW?

Only around 5% of the world's oceans have been explored.

1 Great white shark

2 Manatee

3 Common octopuses

4 Marlins

5 Thresher sharks

6 Hammerhead sharks

7 Swordfish

8 Bottlenose dolphins

THRESHER SHARK

Thresher sharks get their name because of their large tail, which looks like a thresher. A thresher is a name for a long hook-like blade.

LET'S GO!

Can you guess how hammerhead sharks got their name?

HAMMERHEAD SHARK

Hammerhead sharks are great hunters. They have wide heads that give them a better range of sight compared to other sharks. Hammerhead sharks also use their heads to pin prey to the sea floor.

BOTTLENOSE DOLPHIN

Bottlenose dolphins are intelligent hunters. They like to swim in groups. They are playful and fast, working together to prey on schools of fish.

COMMON OCTOPUS

Common octopuses have a large head and eight arms! Each arm is covered in suckers. The suckers can be used to grip objects from the sea floor.

BASKING SHARKS feed near the surface. They look as though they are basking in the sun, which is where they get their name from. Basking sharks have huge mouths that they use to filter food out of the water.

LET'S GO!

A great white shark can have up to 300 teeth! How many teeth do you have?

GREAT WHITE SHARK

Great white sharks are the largest hunting fish in the ocean. Their super sense of smell helps them to detect blood from miles away.

LET'S GO!

How many types of shark can you name in 30 seconds?

SAILFISH are very fast swimmers. Their name comes from the crests that run the length of their bodies, which look like sails!

MANATEE

Manatees are large blobby creatures also known as sea cows (though they are actually more closely related to elephants). Despite their size, they are very good at swimming and are elegant in the water.

SWORDFISH

Swordfish are large, quick hunters. Their famous sword-like snout can be used to slash at their prey to stun them for a quick and easy meal.

MARLIN

Marlins are some of the biggest and fastest fish in the sea. There are many different types of marlin, from the massive black marlins to the smaller white marlins.

LET'S GO!

Marlins can jump very high. How high can you jump? Take a leap off the ground and see...

The Icy
ARCTIC OCEAN

The Arctic Ocean is the world's most northerly ocean. It is also the smallest and coldest. Although small, its icy water is packed with wildlife such as whales and walruses.

DID YOU KNOW?

Climate change warms the Arctic more than anywhere else on Earth.

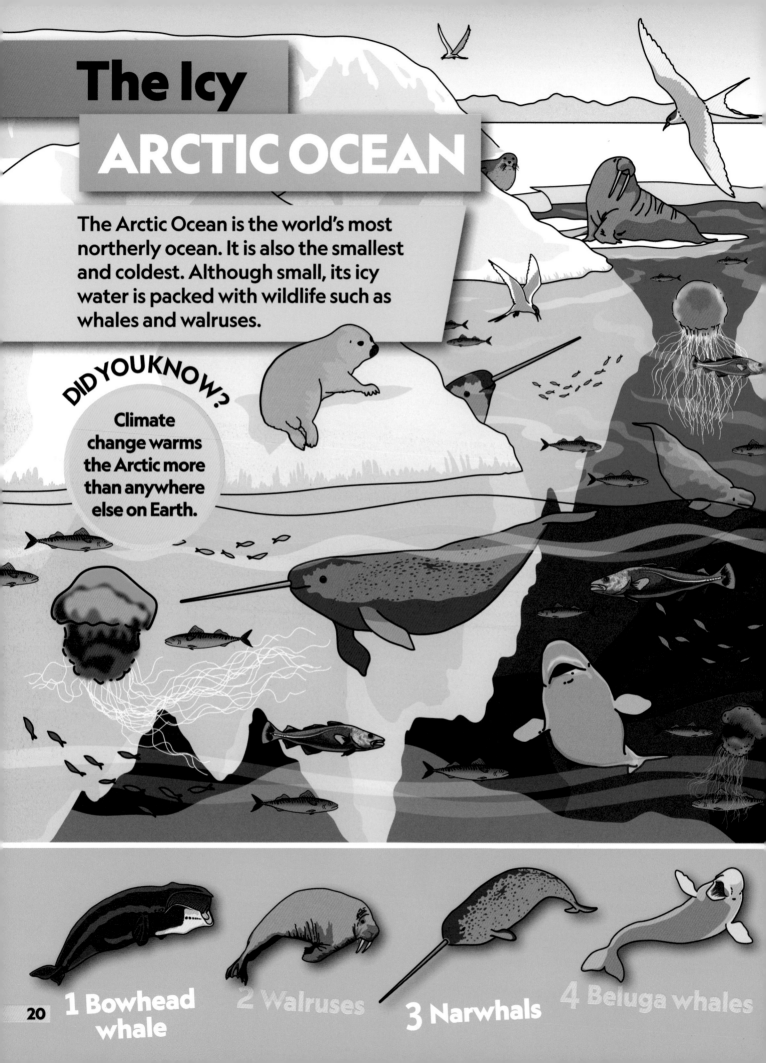

1 Bowhead whale

2 Walruses

3 Narwhals

4 Beluga whales

5 Lion's mane jellyfish

6 Harp seals

7 Arctic cod

8 Arctic tern

21

ARCTIC TERN

Arctic terns have the longest migration (movement from one area to another) of any animal. They fly from the Arctic to Antarctica and back again each year.

ARCTIC COD

Arctic cod are large fish that are common in Arctic waters. They have a substance in their blood, which stops their bodies from freezing solid!

HARP SEAL

Harp seals don't spend much time on shore – they much prefer to swim. They can stay underwater for 15 minutes at a time.

LION'S MANE JELLYFISH

LET'S GO!

Why do you think it's called a jellyfish?

Lion's mane jellyfish are one of the largest jellyfish in the ocean. Their bodies can reach 2 m in width and their tentacles can stretch as long as 36 m (about the length of 9 cars)!

POLAR BEARS are the biggest land carnivores (meat-eaters) in the world. Their blubber (a layer of fat) and thick coat keeps them warm in Arctic temperatures. Their fur also acts as excellent camouflage, helping them blend in with snow and ice.

NARWHAL

Narwhals are a kind of whale. Male narwhals (and some females) have a single tusk that comes out of their head. The tusks are filled with nerves that help narwhals detect changes in their environment.

LET'S GO!

Why do you think narwhals get called 'unicorns of the sea'?

WALRUS

Walruses are huge! Both males and females have long tusks that are used to pull their big bodies out of the water. Walruses also use their tusks to break holes in the ice from below to help them breathe.

BOWHEAD WHALE

Bowhead whales are named after their massive bow-shaped mouth that makes them look as though they are smiling! Like powerful battering rams, they can smash through ice to make breathing holes.

BELUGA WHALE

Beluga whales look like large white dolphins with big round heads. Unlike most other whales, beluga whales can turn their neck in all directions.

LET'S GO!

Beluga whales can swim backwards – can you walk backwards? Remember to look where you are going!

ORCAS are some of the most intelligent predators on earth. They are capable of snatching seals from floating pieces of ice and they can eat over 200 kg of food a day!

The Tropical
INDIAN OCEAN

The Indian Ocean is the warmest ocean on Earth. Found between Africa, Asia and Oceania, these tropical blue waters are home to rays, turtles and a whole lot more...

1 ... back

2 Reef sharks

3 Green ...turtles

4 Giant ...

Find it!

DID YOU KNOW?

Rising sea levels could cause some islands in the Indian Ocean to disappear.

5 Manta

6 Indian Ocean ~~humpback dolphins~~

7 Moray eels

8 Barracudas

27

MANTA RAY

Manta rays are the biggest species of ray. They have huge gaping mouths to gulp in plankton (the fish they eat). Manta rays are nicknamed 'devil fish' because they have horn-shaped fins on the top of their heads.

MORAY EEL

Moray eels are predators with long and often colourful bodies. Some species have toxic mucus (a slimy substance) covering their bodies. Their bite can be dangerous if a human gets too close.

BARRACUDA

Barracudas are speedy swimmers with a torpedo-shaped body. Some of a barracuda's teeth point backwards to stop any fish they catch escaping.

INDIAN OCEAN HUMPBACK DOLPHIN

Indian Ocean humpback dolphins have a small triangle-shaped fin on their hump. They are endangered, meaning there are few left on the planet.

WHALE SHARKS are the biggest fish in the sea and can reach up to 12 m long (about the length of 3 cars)! They are gentle giants and have even been known to let swimmers hitch a ride!

LET'S GO!

Whale sharks are huge! What's the biggest animal you've seen in real life?

LEATHERBACK TURTLE

Leatherback turtles are the biggest turtles on Earth, weighing more than 11 adults! They have long flippers and are excellent swimmers. Their shells are made up of a leathery hide and small sheets of bone. This is why their shells look like they're made of leather.

LET'S GO!

Can you move like a turtle? Try to make it to the other side of the room on your hands and knees.

GIANT GROUPER

Giant groupers are massive bony fish that can weigh up to 400 kg! That's about the same weight as five adult humans!

GREEN SEA TURTLE

Green sea turtles are very large turtles. They can live as long as 100 years! Unlike land turtles, they cannot retract (draw back) into their shell.

REEF SHARK

Reef sharks are medium sized grey sharks that mainly eat small fish. They can smell injured and healthy fish and are very effective predators.

LET'S GO!

Look at all the sharks in this book. Which type is your favourite and why?

Exploring ROCK POOLS

Rock pools are pockets of water that are left behind on the beach when the tide goes out. Creatures like crabs and lobsters have adapted to life on land and in shallow water because of rock pools.

1 Lobster

2 Rock gobies

3 Oystercatchers

4 Hermit crabs

DID YOU KNOW?

The force of gravity from the Sun and Moon creates tides.

5 Molluscs   **6 Urchins**   **7 Sea stars**   **8 Crabs**

SEA STAR

Sea stars are strange animals that have no brains or blood. They are invertebrates, which means they don't have a backbone. They have hundreds of tiny feet that help them move slowly around rocks.

LET'S GO!

Stretch out your arms and legs really wide and make yourself into a human sea star.

LIMPETS are shelled creatures that grip tightly onto rocks. Some limpets have a home spot where they return to when the tide comes in. This is because over time their shell grows to fit the rock more tightly so they aren't swept out to sea.

LET'S GO!

Crabs walk sideways. Can you walk sideways around the room?

E

WHELK

Whelks are the largest of all sea snails in the United Kingdom. They have tall cone-shape shells with wavy patterns.

URCHIN

Some sea urchins are very poisonous and have dangerous spikes poking out in all directions.

COMMON CRAB

Crabs are decapods, which means that they have 10 feet. They sometimes shed these feet, but they are able to grow them back!

LET'S GO!

One family of hermit crabs are all right handed, and another are all left handed. Try writing your name with your 'wrong' hand.

HERMIT CRAB

Hermit crabs are not actually crabs, because they cannot form their own shell. Instead they borrow shells from other animals like whelks and sea snails – really anything they can get their pincers on!

COMMON CUTTLEFISH can control how they float and what colour they are. Baby cuttlefish use their tentacles to walk along the seafloor!

OYSTERCATCHER

Oystercatchers have long colourful beaks that they use to open shellfish. They have white markings on their wings, which makes them easier to spot.

COMMON GOBY

Common gobies are small fish with a sandy colouring. When they lay eggs, the males guard them very protectively.

LOBSTER

Lobsters have long tails and big claws. They never stop growing. Lobsters are known for having long lives, with some species living for over 100 years.

LET'S GO!

Can you rearrange the letters below to make the name of another animal with claws?

B R A C

Creatures
OF THE DEEP

There are many places in the ocean that are so deep even light can't reach. Here, mysterious fish move about in the gloom. With parts of the ocean being so deep and difficult to explore, much of the ocean's mysteries are still waiting to be discovered.

1 Cookiecutter shark

2 Deep sea viperfish

3 Deep sea cucumbers

4 Dumbo octopuses

DID YOU KNOW?

The deepest known part of the ocean is called Challenger Deep. It is almost 11 km below the surface.

5 Cusk eels

6 Fangtooths

7 Gulper eels

8 Deep sea anglerfish

DEEP SEA ANGLERFISH

Anglerfish have long needle-like teeth and even bigger mouths! Females also have fleshy bulbs that come over their heads to light up the dark waters. These bulbs attract small fish that are then swallowed up in one big bite!

DEEP SEA HATCHETFISH

have faces that are squashed onto strange bodies that are shaped like a hatchet (a small axe).

LET'S GO!

Deep sea hatchetfish have scrunched up faces – can you pull the funniest face you can?

GULPER EEL

Gulper eels are long thin eels with mouths that look too big for their bodies. They swim with their mouths open to catch crabs and small shrimp.

CUSK EEL

Cusk eels are not true eels because they have fins just below their head called 'ventral' fins. They also have whiskers that come out from under their mouths to help them sense food.

FANGTOOTH

The fangtooth is an aggressive predator. Their fangs are so big that they are unable to fully close their mouth.

41

DUMBO OCTOPUS

Dumbo octopuses are little creatures that measure, on average, only 20 to 30 cm long. They're unique because they live deeper down than any other type of octopus and use their fins to move instead of jets of water.

MEGAMOUTH SHARKS have huge jaws that they keep open while they swim along, letting food swim right into their mouths! Megamouth sharks are extremely rare with very few ever seen in the wild.

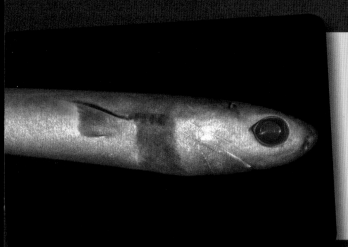

COOKIECUTTER SHARK

Cookiecutter sharks are small sharks, growing to around 50 cm. They feed on larger animals by latching onto them and taking circle-shaped bites from their flesh.

DEEP SEA VIPERFISH

The deep sea viperfish is one of the most terrifying fish around! They use their massive teeth to pierce their prey which they swallow whole.

LET'S GO!

Can you push out your bottom jaw and make your best viperfish face?

DEEP SEA CUCUMBER

Deep sea cucumbers are like the ocean's answer to earthworms! They recycle waste and dead matter for smaller animals. The sea cucumbers that live in the deepest parts of the ocean have adapted to light up!

SOLUTIONS
The Precious Pacific Ocean

The Super Southern Ocean

The Amazing Atlantic Ocean

The Icy Arctic Ocean

The Tropical Indian Ocean

Exploring Rock pools

Magnifying glass game

Penguin

Published by Collins
An imprint of HarperCollins Publishers
Westerhill Road
Bishopbriggs
Glasgow G64 2QT
www.harpercollins.co.uk

HarperCollins Publishers
Macken House, 39/40 Mayor Street Upper, Dublin 1, D01 C9W8, Ireland

In association with National Geographic Partners, LLC

NATIONAL GEOGRAPHIC and the Yellow Border Design are trademarks of the National Geographic Society, used under license.

First published 2021

ISBN
978-0-00-842189-2
978-0-00-865203-6

10 9 8 7 6 5 4 3 2 1

A catalogue record for this book is available from the British Library

Printed in UAE.

If you would like to comment on any aspect of this book,
please contact us at the above address or online.
natgeokidsbooks.co.uk
collins.reference@harpercollins.co.uk

Paper from responsible sources.

Acknowledgements
Illustrations by Steve Evans

Images
P24 narwhal © All Canada Photos/Alamy Stock Photo; P24 bowhead whale © elvin Aitken /VWPics/Alamy Stock Photo; P29 Indian humpback dolphin © Terry Whittaker/Flpa/ imageBROKER/Shutterstock; P40 deep sea anglerfish © Solvin Zankl/Alamy Stock Photo; P41 gulper eel © Adisha Pramod/Alamy Stock Photo; P41 cusk eel © disha Pramod/Alamy Stock Photo; P41 fangtooth © Paulo Oliveira/Alamy Stock Photo; P42 dumbo octopus © NOAA/Alamy Stock Photo; P43 cookiecutter shark © Blue Planet Archive/Alamy Stock Photo; P43 deep sea viperfish © Nature Picture Library/Alamy Stock Photo; P43 deep sea cucumber © Nature Picture Library/Alamy Stock Photo

All other images © Shutterstock.com